Love, Pueo

A Journey Through Loss, Grief and Finding Life Again

Briar Simon

PKL Press

Contents

Dedication

This book is dedicated to the girl who has my heart forever. Until we meet again. I will always love you more than the sun, the moon, and all the stars in the sky.

A letter to my former self

Dear Briar,

Today is Saturday, December 9th, 2023 and tomorrow you will lose Pueo. One minute she will be here, laying right in front of you, and just a few short hours later she will be gone. Her death will shock you, shatter you, and crush you, but you will survive.

For months you will ask yourself how you missed the signs and symptoms, but in reality, they were never there. You will ask why a million times and there will be no answer. Why couldn't I have a last day with her? Why did this happen? Why, why, why, why. What if, what if, what if. None of these questions will serve you. You will cry and scream and feel nothing and everything all at the same time.

You will feel crazy, like you have lost your mind and that you will never think clearly again. You will absolutely lose yourself.

But one day you will begin picking up the pieces. It won't be perfect that's for sure. You will mess up, hurt the ones you love, and make choices you cannot take back; but it will all iron itself out. You will become a softer and more empathetic version of yourself. A person you have truly always wanted to be. It turns out, you can be authentic and hardened while also showing emotion, and it does not make you weak. You'll learn that in fact it is quite the opposite.

You will miss her every single day.

If you look down right now, you will see your girl teasing your boy with a ball. That boy? He will become your best friend, your entire heart. He will lie with you every day as you cry, he will be your strength, your compass, your light. Right now as I write this, he has recently turned eight. Watching him age and living in fear will be hard, but he is the reason that I am able to write you this letter. He will carry you.

One day you will meet Lucy and I won't spoil anything for you except, she's yours now. I am writing this to you on her one year adoption anniversary.

You and Andrew are fine. Kekoa is fine. Lucy is fine. Most importantly, you are fine.

There will still be a gaping hole in your chest. You'll feel it every day. But you'll finally write, you'll finally help others in a way that matters, you'll find your people, you will listen to more Bayside than you ever thought imaginable, but you will survive it. I wish this did not happen to us and I still don't exactly understand why it did and we never will.

You will make it to the other side, I promise.

Love,

Future Briar

Pueo: Loss

poo-eh-oh

Learning to let go, and carry love beyond goodbye

Introduction

Love, Pueo is a compilation of essays written in the two years after losing my best friend and the love of my life. When Pueo died in December 2023, my world shattered. The day after she suddenly died, I took my mom to Barnes & Noble and I searched for every book on grief I could find. I desperately needed a road map to help me navigate this pain of suddenly losing my soul dog. While it's no surprise that there is no road map, it was surprising how few books and resources exist for pet loss.

After a year of grieving, healing, falling apart and trying my best to put it all back together again, I decided to put my words into the world, hoping to reach even one person. At first I started a blog with the same name as this book. After a few months of writing and receiving feedback, I decided to pursue a lifelong dream, which is what you are holding in your hands.

I have always wanted to be a published writer and turning my love for Pueo into something beautiful and meaningful is more than I ever could have imagined coming from her death.

The process was long and difficult, it required taking breaks, sometimes month long breaks. It required opening up and being vulnerable enough to put my work into the world for all to see and critique. I had to overcome severe imposter syndrome and remind myself constantly that my story, her story, is worth telling. At the end of it all, I had to honor myself, my journey, my emotions and my needs over everything else. Doing so allowed me to create something I am truly proud of.

If you are reading this, I hope my words help you understand you are not alone and you are never alone. Grief is messy and complicated and misunderstood and hard. If you are reading this, I have to assume you love your animal companion deep in the depths of your soul. Maybe right now it feels like you will never be able to live or breathe without them. I see you. I have been you and some days I still am you.

These essays are messy and raw and honest. They are the light and the darkness that lives within us after losing a piece of ourselves. They helped heal pieces of me and I hope they can help heal pieces of you too.

The three parts are each named after one of the dogs in this journey, and represent what that dog has taught me. Pueo taught me about loss, Kekoa taught me about strength, and Lucy taught me about resilience. Sometimes the content may be repetitive. Stories may be told more than once, and some stories may be less about the journey and more about the dog. They are certainly not in chronological order, because there is no timeline to grief anyway.

I wrote this book so that it feels like you're hearing from a friend, and I hope it reads that way for you, too.

A Love Letter to Pueo

Pueo,

The closest feeling I will ever have to holding my newborn baby is when you were handed to me for the first time. I immediately loved you. The entire drive home, you cried and tilted your head to Mac Miller's "Knock Knock" and showed me your little seven week old personality.

That first year was truly me and you against the world. You were my shadow and my fiercest protector. Growing up, I always felt unsafe. I thought I would never experience unconditional love and stability. Those things were for others, not for me. You taught me I was worthy. Any time we went out in public, you dutifully sat behind me, watching my back, protecting me and waiting for our next move. When I got my Pueo owl tattooed on my arm, I made sure to place it in a way that when I stood up with my arms down, the owl was facing behind me. Then you could have my back forever.

Through the years, we took turns protecting each other. When a big storm came through, it was my turn. You'd run to the closet or the back of the bed, scared, and I was always there to hold you through it. Through this, we became completely intertwined, like one soul within two bodies. You always knew I was going to have an anxiety attack before I knew because we were completely in sync with one another.

When you were about a year and a half old, we welcomed your daddy into our lives. You were not thrilled with the prospect. For two weeks, every time he would leave and enter the room, even just to go to the bathroom, you barked at him. I guess it was your attempt to scare him away from us and keep him out of your spot on the bed. Eventually, you warmed up and welcomed him into our pack. Now, he loves you just as much as I do.

Through it all, you took everything in stride. You adapted to whatever life threw at us. Together, we moved from New Jersey to Kansas, back again, and then to where we are now. You were always the same happy girl. You made new friends in Nicolette and Chief, learning how to gently play with small dogs. You welcomed Kekoa and truly treated him like a little brother.

When you left this physical world, my reality shattered. Everything felt broken. To be honest, it still does most days. Two years later, I still feel the pain in my chest, and the hole in my heart. It feels as fresh as the day you left.

But you never really left, did you?

I feel you every day in the wind, in the stars, in my chest. Some days I still see you as if you are popping by to say hello. I talk to you and I have heard you talk back. I have asked you for guidance when we were losing Libby, D.O.G, Pretzel, Beanie, and so many others. You always knew what was going to happen before anyone else. You told me through energy and a feeling in my chest.

You may not physically be here, but your spirit is always with me. When I ask for a sign, you always provide one. You are my guardian angel, my light in the darkness. You are the first one I will look for when it is my time to go into the light. I do not know if there is an afterlife, but I have to believe in one because I have to see you again one day.

You were my everything. You are my everything. I love you forever.

Love, Pueo

As described in the introduction, Love, Pueo began as a blog and this is the post that started it all.

Today is my birthday, January 26th, 2025. As I do every year, I have reflected on the last year of my life, a year markedly defined by grief. On December 10th, 2023, we lost my soulmate, my best friend, my other half, Pueo. We lost her suddenly, without warning, and at only 8 years old.

Grief defined me.

I walked into 33 deeply hurt, traumatized, and unable to see a future without her, unable to imagine moving forward. I spent the year in acute grief and I allowed myself to feel every single moment of the pain. I navigated through the year with Kekoa and Andrew by my side. I reconnected with people who I could not have survived without, and disconnected from those who no longer served me. I spent every day missing her, yearning for her, loving her.

As I enter 34, I want to turn my pain into passion in the hopes of helping others. Sharing my experience, continuing to grieve and to learn about grief, and continuing to be vulnerable.

Love, Pueo is a blog about love, loss and grief, and all the obstacles along the way.

December 10, 2023

Trigger warning: this post discusses pet death and heman-giosarcoma.

"Poo what are you doing?"

I asked her while laughing. She was such a silly girl, what was she doing hiding behind the Peloton? Maybe there was lightning? I was watching television with headphones on so I didn't hear anything.

She comes out from behind the Peloton and her back legs give out. *Here we go, hip dysplasia* I thought.

Immediately we carry her to the bedroom and I start to cry. Something's wrong. Something's wrong. Something's wrong. I could feel it in my gut, in my core.

It's 5 pm and I call my mom. Pueo is lethargic. Mom says "I'm sure she's fine, she probably slept on her legs wrong and it freaked her out"

Okay. She's right. But she's not right. Maybe I'll just call the ER vet.

"Hi, my dogs legs just gave out from under her and she seems pretty lethargic" they say "just monitor her and bring her in if anything gets worse"

Okay well it's probably fine. It's not, but maybe it is.

My stomach starts acting up, anxiety, IBS. It's really not the time for this.

We grab a towel and we place her on the floor. We wrap the towel under her to support her in walking to the living room. She walks. She walks perfectly to her bed and lays down. *Okay. Mom was right.*

Andrew grabs me a pillow and blanket so I can continue watching "Married at First Sight" while laying near her. Laying near her isn't enough, I need to lay in bed with her and make sure she knows it's all okay, and mamas here.

Her breathing starts to get labored.

"Andrew, we have to take her to the vet. Something's not right. I know it. Something's not right."

He resists. The ER is expensive and when it comes to my babies, I tend to be dramatic. Not this time. But I say okay and I keep myself close to her. Feeling her entire body, checking everything to make sure he's right. He's not.

I feel her stomach. Something's not right. It's squishy. Something's not right.

"We have to take her in," I say.

He resigns.

"Okay, well let's go," he replies.

It is pouring rain. He wraps her up in the towel and carries her down the stairs and to the car, nearly dropping her on the way. The time is 6:40. She was 55 pounds, but usually light as a feather. Why was he having trouble carrying her?

We get in the car, I'm driving and he's in the backseat with her. She's not crying. She's trying to get up and laying down but she's not crying. She always cries in the car. Something's wrong.

It's 7:10 and we get to the ER. We pull the car up to the door and they bring out the gurney.

"Her gums are pale," they say.

We go inside and sit down, I start googling "pale gums in dogs" and the first result is heart failure.

There is NO way. She had the zoomies at 2:30. She's only eight. She's always had regular check ups, regular shots. She's always been healthy.

I start to lose track of time.

We are called into the room with the doctor very quickly. This can't be good.

"Pueos condition is critical," she said.

That's all I heard before my brain starts screaming *oh my god. No. Oh my god. No. No. This can't be. No. Oh my god. No. Please no.*

I'm not leaving with her.

She has blood in her abdomen and her heart rate is extremely low. They are trying to stabilize her and can't. If they could stabilize her, further testing would cost us $2500 and surgery would cost $10,000. She would have to be moved to another hospital and because of her vitals, she may not survive the ride.

I look at Andrew and say "go sell my car". The doctor says she will come back so we can have time to think about what we want to do.

I call my grandmother, sobbing. I call my mom, sobbing. I am leaving this hospital without my baby girl.

The doctor comes back and advises us that euthanasia is the only option. She can't be stabilized. I am leaving this hospital without my baby girl. Why is this happening to me.

The time is 8:45 pm and we are moved to a comfort room. A room with couches and essential oils and we are discussing cremation options, keepsakes, all these things I never thought about.

The doctor runs in and says "you have to come with me, she's trying to pass"

We run to be by her side. I kiss her, tell her she will always be my first baby and I love her. I listen to her heart stop. The time is 9:08.

I am shocked.

I am distraught.

I am inconsolable.

I am lost.

I've lost my baby girl.

In the span of four hours, my life changed.

We lost Pueo to hemangiosarcoma (HSA), a disease I had never heard of. It's a very aggressive cancer that forms in the blood vessels. It's difficult to find and one of the symptoms is sudden death. Knowing what I know now, there were signs, but they were subtle. They were nothing to worry about had this disease not been lingering. She was fatigued on walks at night. I chalked it up to her being tired. She didn't want to eat. She was always a fussy eater.

Neither of these symptoms would lead anyone, including the vet, to believe her death was among us. There is a large community for HSA online, Facebook groups and other communities. Just like everything else in grief, we are not alone. HSA is trauma. These stories are traumatic. They can cause — or worsen — Post-Traumatic Stress Disorder. Sudden loss is traumatic, and should be treated as such.

We are not alone.

The Weight of Survival

Trigger warning: this chapter discusses suicide, suicidal ideation, and anti-depressant use.

A few weeks after her death, the support subsided. People generally could not handle my overwhelming sadness and I couldn't either. I was in therapy and I built a good support system for myself, but I still did not know who my grief was safe with and who it was not.

The world moved on while mine stood completely still. I lived every day in this grief-ridden body, crying so loud that my neighbor once asked me "Did you adopt a dog?"

I said no.

"Oh," she replied, "I thought I heard a small dog whimpering."

It was me. I was the small dog she heard, except I was not whimpering, I was full on sobbing uncontrollably. Every. Single. Day.

For the first few weeks, I saw my therapist twice per week. Then once a week for months, but it wasn't enough. Plain and simple, if she wasn't in this world, I didn't want to be either. I didn't know how to carry on, how to go back to some form of normalcy, I just wanted to be with her again.

Every day I woke up was a curse. I begged the world, please, just take me like you took her.

With each passing day, the urge to take my own life grew. The more time that passed from when she was last on Earth, the worse I felt. I would write about it online as a cry for help. I would talk about it openly. I talked about having a plan and still no one took me seriously.

One night, I guess people started paying attention.

My aunt contacted my mom about one of my Facebook posts that read, "I wish I died when she did. I can't do this." At the time, that is how I genuinely felt.

This spun my mom into a spiral and she thought I needed to be checked into an inpatient facility.

My mom had my stepdad, the man who raised me, but could never get a handle on my emotions, call me to see why I was so upset. The conversation was a lot of dismissing my feelings and reminding me that I knew she would not live that long. He kept saying "the dog" instead of her name until I snapped and demanded that he call her Pueo. It was a lot of me explaining why I felt alone. Everyone was concerned, except the loudest ones never reached out to me, never contributed to or shared my GoFundMe. Nothing. It felt like my family used it as a gossip piece rather than genuine concern.

Bless his heart, he tried. This was never a task he should have been put up to. But there I was, just two months after her death, being completely misunderstood and more alone than ever.

A week or so later, my mom tried. She told me I needed to stop posting "this shit" on Facebook and I refused.

"I can post whatever the fuck I want on my own Facebook and people can say they're concerned, but no one has reached out."

She said I was being dramatic.

In hindsight, do I understand her point? Yes, I do. I was never actually going to take my own life, but I was desperately seeking validation.

I wanted support, I needed support.

Before she died, I was taking .25 mg of Xanax at night to help me sleep and 150 mg of Wellbutrin every morning. Within a few weeks, I was taking .5 mg of Xanax and 450 mg of Wellbutrin. The medication was the only way to keep the suicidal ideations at bay.

I took .5 mg of Xanax every single day to be able to fall asleep and sometimes that wasn't even enough. I would still have heart palpitations or anxiety that kept me up all night.

Sometimes I would have to add melatonin to the mix. I hoped the raise in medication would be a temporary fix. Just for a few months. I was so embarrassed by how much medication I needed, I never wanted to talk about it. Now I feel differently.

The medication kept me alive without dulling my emotions. I needed to feel my feelings, otherwise I knew I would absolutely explode. I had lived through that many years before. I felt my feelings, but the medication tamed down the extremity of my depression.

I stayed alive, and that's what mattered.

It is okay to need medication. It is okay to see the therapist. It is okay to cry out for help. It is okay to need help. Do what you have to do to stay alive, because your animal companion would want you to. They love us and they will see us when it is our time, but they want us to continue to grow and love and be better and one day be the new version of ourselves that is born from their death.

We are not alone.

The Firsts

Pueo died two weeks before Christmas and at that point, the tree was up, the gifts were bought. Christmas was happening. I do not recall Christmas 2023, but I am pretty sure I just cried the entire day. Christmas 2024 felt like our real first Christmas without her.

In our house after Christmas comes my husband's birthday, then mine, then Valentine's Day, all in quick succession. We celebrate everything in this house and take birthdays seriously, but not last year.

Turning 33 and leaving her in year 32 felt massive. She was with me since I was 24 years old. I hit milestones with her. 25, then my golden birthday, 26, then 30. 30 was hard for a million reasons, but her strength and joy carried me through a particularly hard time. I couldn't reconcile leaving her in my early 30s, let alone my 30s at all.

For all the firsts that came and went, I did things my way. I set boundaries. Overall, I am glad I did this, but I do have regrets. I refused to acknowledge the first Christmas. No tree, no gifts, nothing. I did not think of how this would affect my husband and my family. I told everyone, "She was MY dog and I can't celebrate without her." I also said, "I was forced to celebrate last year, but I don't want to this year." And, "If I don't have her, no gift will even matter because I lost everything already."

I didn't allow my family to celebrate, just because I didn't want to. I forced the world to stop for everyone else and did not consider the feelings of others, mainly my husband, who also had his world shaken by her death. He wanted things to feel normal and like we could continue, but I could not fathom normalcy. Normalcy was a betrayal. In the end, I hurt my husband deeply by not compromising on how we would spend this first. I refused to acknowledge and validate his needs, which were just as important as mine. Ultimately, I learned a hard lesson in partnership and compromise.

Holidays and birthdays are the obvious firsts that hurt deeply. But they do not warn you about the changing of the seasons. The first snow, the first time the flowers bloom, the first insufferable hot day, and always our favorite, the changing of the leaves. The seasons mark time passing, the world moving forward, even when you are standing still. The snow still falls, the flowers still bloom and the leaves still change even though you're stuck in the moment your world stopped. We don't talk nearly enough about this.

We have now lived through a full year of firsts and I wish I could say holidays hurt less, birthdays hurt less, seasons hurt less, but they just don't.

As I put together Lucy and Kekoa's Easter baskets, I yearned for her. But I honored her. I gave Pueo's Easter basket to Lucy. I bought all their favorite things. Toys, grunting piggies, bones, all of it, but we still have one missing piece. Every milestone without her feels like there is an emptiness. Like she belongs in the room.

To be honest, I hope it stays this way forever. I hope I yearn for her every time I turn a year older and she stays eight years old. Her memory, the void she left in our lives, and the ways we choose to honor her keep her alive. At the end of it all, she would want to celebrate and she would want us to all be happy as a unit.

Do what feels right for you and your family as you move through all the firsts. Take care of yourself and take care of each other.

Grief is grief and hard is hard

It's been seventeen months since I lost Pueo. Seventeen months since my last night with her. Seventeen months since the last time we rolled around on the floor and played ball. For three days before her passing she played keep away from her brother, which was one of her favorite games. She would take his favorite ball and carry it around proudly, never allowing him to have it back. It was like she knew what was to come, but I didn't know it was our last night together because the universe stole her from me so suddenly.

Over the last seventeen months, I have met so many grieving pet parents. Some had babies who had long battles with cancer or other illnesses. Some who have lost their babies suddenly, tragically, like we lost Pueo or in accidents. I have met people whose pets were so young, like Piper who was only two and I have met people whose pets were 17, like Mitzy, and every age in between.

For a long time, and sometimes still, when I hear of people having 15, 16, 17, etc, years with their babies, I am filled with rage. Anger. I didn't even get ten. It wasn't fair. I felt rage when I heard that people got to have these last days with their pets, last days I only dreamed of. Days doing their dogs favorite things or feeding them chocolate cupcakes.

I felt robbed.

But was I?

The ebb and flow of the anger is persistent, but I have learned that although my loss was sudden and tragic, Pueo never knew a day of sadness. We did not have a long drawn-out battle with hemangiosarcoma (HSA) or any other illness, and for that, I am thankful. If I knew my girl was sick, I wouldn't have spent a single day away from her. How could I?

But many people had to. People I know had to carry on as normally as they could while their loved one was sick and possibly dying. I've met people whose pets lived through month long battles with different diseases, but their lives had to continue as normal. They went to work, celebrated birthdays, went on vacations. Their life could not stop because of the care. They watched their pets struggle, went to endless doctor's appointments and gave countless medications.

So what's better? To never know until they are gone, but never have a sad moment with them? Or to know, but have their last days, months, or years filled with sadness and anticipatory grief?

The answer is neither. Grief and loss don't know "better" or "worse". There are no levels to loss. At the end of the day, our babies are gone. We have a gaping hole in our chest. We yearn for them, cry for them, and miss them every day.

As much as I wanted to scream "YOU GOT THIS AND I DIDN'T," I had to learn that someone would say that about me. Grief is grief. Hard is hard. The journeys are unique, but the end result is all the same.

I have replaced my anger with empathy and understanding. When people say they had more years than I did, I remind myself to be happy for them.

It's all hard. No matter what. We are all in this together.

***

Between the publishing of the blog and the publishing of this book, we lost my grandmother's dog D.O.G and we learned my mom's dog Snoopy has cancer. D.O.G was 14 and a half years old and Snoopy is 13. D.O.G had been declining over the past couple of years and my grandmother has had to go through the process of deciding when it was time to say goodbye. Snoopy's diagnosis is brand new. We are waiting on the call to find out more information about the cancer and the treatment options. This is something my mom will have to move through, manage and make decisions about. I am sure before publishing, there will be an update, I just hope it's not a bad one. I think about these decisions frequently. I do not know how I would have been able to handle a diagnosis. I truly believe I would have bankrupt us to try to save Pueo and with HSA, the survival rate is so low that it probably would have been for nothing.

No matter the outcome with Snoopy, she may be 13, but hard is hard. These choices and decisions are hard. I think sometimes my grandmother feels guilty that she got 14 years and I only had eight, but I have to continue to reassure her that there could never be enough time.

As I sit here and watch Kekoa age, I know the day will come that I have to face this again. I will always say I deserved more time. It is never enough. It could never be enough.

***

Unfortunately, we have learned that Snoopy has melanoma and my mom has decided not to pursue treatment or go through staging with an oncologist. While I also would not proceed with treatment at her age, I do wish she was going through staging so we could have a better idea of how much time we have. As of today she still has plenty of energy and shows no signs of slowing down. We know the day is coming so for now, we enjoy the time we have left with her, cherish every moment and prepare for the inevitable.

You can't outrun the emptiness

We just came home from seeing *Marvel's The Thunderbolts*. I usually walk into Marvel movies with little to no knowledge, because I am only mildly immersed in the universe. I had no expectations other than excitement to see Bucky Barnes on the big screen.

Marvel movies always have some element of emotion throughout them, but *The Thunderbolts* was riddled with grief from the opening scene.

On the surface, the movie is about a group of misfits who are brought together and forced to work together to escape death. Through this, they bond, becoming something larger than themselves and setting the stage for what comes next. While they are working together, their secrets and trauma come out. Death of a sister, abusive family, and abandonment.

The group meets Bob, who they thought was a civilian until he turned into The Sentry. The most powerful super soldier, whose power is used for evil. He is turned into the darkness hiding inside him. In the lead up to the ending, Bob is fighting The Sentry and becomes uncontrollable. He is trying to kill the darkness through violence, which makes the darkness stronger. More powerful. He becomes the part of himself that he buried deep down. The part of himself he wouldn't share with anyone. The part who told him he was alone.

His spell couldn't be broken until the group came together, hugged Bob, and pulled him from the darkness, reminding him that he was okay and not alone.

Grief can make us feel like we are completely alone. After Pueo died, I felt like I was on my own island and I refused to let those closest to me in. I wouldn't open up to my family. I was unreasonable, cruel, selfish, alone, dark.

That's what the darkness does to us if we allow it to. If we give power to grief, give power to the darkness, the darkness becomes us and can become us until we lose everything and everyone.

I have personally seen grief destroy people. Diminish their light. Their new normal became hatred, jealousy and rage, and even years later they never regained their shine.

Feel the grief. Embrace your dark days. Accept that some days you will feel alone, but you are not always alone and you don't have to let the darkness overcome you. If you have family or friends who have lost, grief can be a powerful bonding tool. If you do not have a safe space of family or friends, try support groups. Try chat rooms and Facebook groups. Open yourself up and talk about your grief, talk about your loved one.

We cannot outrun the emptiness in our hearts.

We don't have to let the darkness become us. We are not alone. We are not misfits. Maybe we just have yet to find our fit.

I have added resources I have used to the back of the book. Please reach out for help if you need it. You are not alone.

Complicated Grief

As I write this, I am sitting, staring at photos of Pueo. I have a few of my favorite photos of her taped to my computer monitor at work, and from time to time I find myself just staring at them. Hardly processing, hardly thinking. The brain really just shuts off.

The past few weeks have felt unnecessarily difficult. I find myself thinking of her all the time, but I cannot figure out what I am even thinking. It's just this... missing. Longing. Wishing. Remembering.

A few months into my grief, I felt crazy. I felt like I was never getting better and my therapist said, "Within a year is acute grief. If this lasts longer than a year, we will have to discuss at that time." About eight months into my loss, I stopped going to therapy. It felt like every session I was just reopening the wound. It became just a space to talk about my pain, but somehow it was making it more painful. I walked out feeling worse than when I walked in.

So now, this complicated and prolonged grief just sits inside me. It sits on me like a slab on my chest. I can't breathe. I can't move. I am not crying. I am not doing anything but sitting still, feeling paralyzed.

Over the last few weeks, I have been pushing this sadness down. As someone who has been very open and honest about my grief, this was not the norm for me. I wouldn't admit it and I have no idea why. I didn't open up to my best friends, my husband, or anyone, and I was hardly willing to admit it to myself.

That was until my husband and I started talking about her and talking about how much we missed her. I said "I've been really sad lately," to which he replied, "I could tell your energy was different, but I figured you'd talk when you were ready."

I swear the man lives in my brain. That's the exact response I needed, and that's exactly what I wanted him to do. I didn't want to open up, talk about it, or think about it. Some days it's all too much. But I think that's normal.

I mean, do you ever stop missing your loved ones? Do you ever stop loving them? Is complicated grief as bad as the experts make it sound? Is it not normal?

One day, when the time is right, I will go back to therapy, but for now, I am going to continue my sadness and grief.

But I will go back to expressing my emotions to family and friends.

So long as the sadness isn't impeding my daily life, it feels normal to me.

Compound Grief

In the midst of losing Pueo, my husband and I were also grieving his grandmother. Less than three months prior to losing Pueo, we learned his grandmother had pancreatic cancer. Like hemangiosarcoma, it is a very aggressive cancer, and we knew we did not have much time. Just four weeks later, we lost her.

So when we added grief to grief, it became difficult to process any of it. The loss of grandma was intertwined with the loss of Pueo. The grief overwhelmed us to the point that we could not separate the two, it all just felt like chaos in our brains.

His family lives across the country from us and as we were driving out to say our goodbyes, she passed 8 hours into our 21 hour drive. Being in the house where she lived and died, where we lived with her for a short period of time, and where we had hundreds of memories with her, was almost haunting.

In the week we were there, he filled a suitcase with belongings of hers that he wanted and he felt would keep her close forever.

When we came home, we put the suitcase to the side until he could process the emotions, and was ready to go through everything and find a proper space for the items.

A few weeks later, Pueo died and the suitcase and its belongings still sit under his desk. Losing Pueo was in our face every day, from the time we woke up to the time we went to sleep. We felt her absence constantly, whereas grandma's loss did not hit us in the same immediate way.

Grieving grandma was pushed to the side, and it would end up resurfacing randomly. When his mom sounded like her, when Kekoa would spin and spin to lay down (since she always commented on it), or when we would FaceTime his parents and he could no longer say hi to her.

The compound grief made him shut down, not want to deal with any of the grief, and not want to see any reminders of them. Eventually, the emotions bubbled to the surface and he has been forced to grieve them both. We are over two years into these massive losses and he finally feels like he is able to grieve grandma more actively instead of just grieving Pueo.

Compound grief is very difficult to manage and navigate and we are still learning lessons from this concept. Experiencing multiple losses in a short time frame is a form of trauma, and should be treated as such. If you are experiencing compound grief, you are not alone and there are ways through the block in your brain.

Heart Dog

I never heard of the term "heart dog" until Pueo died. I knew our bond was special, of course. I knew she grounded me. I knew her loss felt deeper than just something missing. It felt like an amputation. As if someone came in, cut out my heart and left a gaping hole, but somehow I was still breathing.

In the days that followed her death, I searched for every resource possible. I needed something to help me feel better. I needed to feel okay because I couldn't bear the pain, I needed it to be manageable. As I now know, that is impossible. There could never be enough resources to help the pain, the only resource that helps is time.

However, I did find one book called *Heart Dog: Surviving the Loss of Your Canine Soulmate* by Roxanne Hawn. This book helped everything click into place. Pueo was my soulmate, the love of my life, and the one special dog I'd have forever. The book put into perspective why I was (and still am) in so much pain from the loss and that my prolonged grief was perfectly normal. Pueo was not just a dog. She was my anchor and a piece of my central nervous system.

It's okay to cry for years, it's okay to never have the same soulmate connection with another dog, it's okay that it feels like an amputation.

Every dog we have, we love differently because they all serve different purposes, and they come into our lives at different times. Loving each dog has deepened my understanding of why Pueo is my heart dog.

Pueo was the first dog who was mine. She was my right hand, my protector, my guardian. She taught me about unconditional love. She was there when I met my husband and walked me down the aisle when we got married. We moved twice together, went through so many ups and downs and through it all, we were stuck together like glue. From the day she came home, we were completely inseparable.

Kekoa is my sweet little baby. Stoic and protective when he has to be, and he's filled his big sister's shoes as my shadow. He will always be the first dog my husband and I got together. Kekoa is like a warm blanket on a cold day.

And Lucy. Lucy will always be the dog my heart dog sent me. She's Pueo reincarnated, but less of a protector, and more of a challenger. She challenges me every day. Tests my patience and resilience. She's what I needed to break through in my depression and keep me active and keep me motivated.

All three of my dogs are special, meaningful, incredible and I love them each differently. But there is only one heart dog. And that's okay.

Pueo is my soulmate and it's okay that I mourn her every day. Heart dogs are real. They are different, they are special, and we may only ever have one or we may have many.

I believe she is my one and only.

***

Since the original writing, I have reflected a lot on heart dogs, soul dogs, once in a lifetime dogs, etc. Pueo is definitively my soul twin and the dog who understood me like no one else. Our connection is deeper than a heart dog connection. Since she has been gone, I can still feel her presence, like her spirit follows me around. I can channel her, ask her for signs, ask for guidance and I feel her answers in my chest. She owns a piece of my soul and our connection will live on forever.

Over the last two years, I have accepted that Kekoa is my heart dog. He is my emotional center and has taught me how to love deeper. He truly owns my heart. When he looks at me, it is as if I can feel our hearts connecting.

It is a very different love and not something that is even comparable to Pueo. I feel so lucky that I can have both a heart dog and a soul dog and I believe that you can have both and you can have multiple. How lucky are we as humans to have these animals in our lives who connect with us on the deepest of levels?

Pueo may still always be my one soul dog, but who knows. Maybe one day there will be another dog who is destined for me. Maybe I will be that lucky.

Love, Pueo & Libby

In April 2025, my best friend lost her dog Libby. Losing Libby also felt like a loss for me and made me reflect on everything my friend now has to deal with.

Like me, they live in an apartment, which means a lot of outdoor interaction with neighbors and people who have met your dog or have seen your dog for years. And one day they're just...gone.

My friend and I shared a similar loss journey. Libby and Pueo were around the same age, Libby was nine and Pueo was eight. They did not grow old, and they were not sick for long. Seemingly, they were here and healthy one day, and gone the next.

For us, Pueo was the loudest one in the neighborhood. She barked at everything and everyone, so not only was her loss visible, it was audible. For months I had to wear a hoodie with noise canceling headphones so if anyone talked to me, I could easily ignore them. It took me months to be able to tell other people that she was gone, and I would have never acknowledged it if I was not asked. I acted as if they just did not see her.

I remember one day six months after Pueo's death, as I was heading to work, a woman who lived near me asked, "what happened to your black and white dog?" I told her. Her response was "I noticed it had been quieter outside." This nearly broke me, nearly made me crawl into a ball and never come outside again. Pueo's silence was not only in my world, but others as well. Neighbors stopped seeing her, stopped hearing her and noticed.

As the weather got warmer and people came outside more, I was asked what happened more often.

But one day I had a realization. How special is it that she lives in the minds of others? She was not just mine, she was part of the community. Her being gone was as much of a shock to others as it was to me. People have offered sympathy, and remember her.

Just recently, one neighbor told me he missed her. I miss her every day, but even almost a year and a half later, others in my community miss her, too.

Every day is difficult without her. Every day when I walk Lucy, I think about if people are curious about what happened to Pueo. The reminders of her absence used to hurt me and made me nervous to ask about others' losses, but now I realize that all a griever wants is for their loved ones to be remembered, be loved, be missed. Often in grief, it feels as if the world moves on while yours stands still. You stand still in your grief, wishing they were here, and feeling like the world forgot.

The world didn't forget.

Just like I learned my community never forgot Pueo, I hope my best friend knows her community will never forget, and I hope she sees the beauty in this. The beauty in Libby living forever in the minds of others. I hope we can all remember that our dogs were loved, seen, heard and cherished by many. Because of this, they live forever.

The stages

They say there are five stages of grief, but stages typically imply a linear progression, and grief is anything but linear.

I skipped denial entirely. There was no space for it. She was here and then she wasn't, and my body understood that before my mind could try to protect me from it. Instead, I replaced denial with guilt.

Some days the guilt is so strong, it makes me nauseous. The anger becomes so intense that another driver not using their blinker can send me into a tailspin. The depression sneaks up on me and sends me to bed for days. As for bargaining, well, I am always bargaining. The number of times I have begged and pleaded with a god I don't believe in to please just bring her back. I will do anything. Give anything. I still beg the universe for a time machine. Please let me go back to the day I got her and live those eight years over again.

Even acceptance isn't linear. Some days I accept that she is gone. There is nothing I could've done differently. There is no way for her to come back. Some days I lay in bed and cry all day. I yearn, and I beg, and I plead. I get mad, at myself, at others, and at the universe. Some days I feel all five "stages" in a single day.

This is my interpretation of grief, with each "stage" as an underlying theme in each chapter.

Accepting bargaining.

Accepting anger.

Accepting depression.

Accepting guilt.

And just accepting. Accepting that acceptance is not permanent.

To the five "stages" of grief I say, you don't exist. Stages aren't real. There is grief and its emotions and there is not grief. Those are the worlds we live in. The stages have only two purposes.

1. Understanding your emotions as you navigate your journey

2. Creating stigma around grief. Allowing those who are not grieving to think grief timelines exist

Just because your loved one is gone, doesn't mean the love goes away. There is no end date to grief. No timeline.

There are no stages, there is just a never-ending roller coaster. As long as we are alive, missing them, and loving them, the grief must exist.

Be kind to yourself.

Be kind to others.

Ebbs and Flows

Grief ebbs and flows as it works its way through my body. Sometimes the grief lands in my heart, sometimes my brain, and sometimes in my entire body. In a few days, it will be 14 months since I lost Pueo. Over a year of crying, yearning, begging, pleading, mental and physical illness, support groups, finding unsafe spaces, relearning who I am, relearning who we are as a family without her, who I am without her, guilt, bargaining, anger, depression, denial, but rarely acceptance.

So it has been over a year now. While the world has kept spinning, my job carried on, my friends moved on, life returned to some semblance of normalcy. But I haven't. For the first few months, I woke up and she was my first thought. Every. Single. Day. Once we adopted Lucy, her and Kekoa became my first thoughts each morning. Other times, my brain just reverted to "Oh F*&k, why is my alarm blaring?" as if a 6:45 a.m. alarm wasn't standard. Now, there are days where maybe I do not think of her until I sit at my desk and look at her picture. On weekends maybe it takes me settling into the couch, coffee in hand, ready to turn on my television show of choice when I look over and see her sitting on the shelf in the space I built for her. There is never a day where I do not think of her. I always feel her, miss her, want her, and love her. Love is eternal and present.

It has been over a year and I am not "over it" or "moved on" as people want you to be. As if a loss causing post-traumatic stress disorder is something you just get over. I refuse to buy into toxic positivity. Toxic positivity shows itself in many ways. Common phrases are, "everything happens for a reason," "they wouldn't want you to be sad," and "at least they didn't suffer."

Toxic positivity causes grievers to shut down, feel like they shouldn't talk about their loved ones anymore, or like they should hide their emotions. Shoveling these ideals down grievers' throats is not only misguided, it is harmful, dismissive and it intensifies guilt and shame. It's not okay.

I am not okay because she did not suffer. I am not causing my grief to worsen by thinking about her and talking about her. I am not okay because I have two healthy, wonderful dogs. I am not okay because what I have is great. I am not okay. And that's okay.

As my life continues, there will be days that are bright, beautiful, no clouds in my brain or my body. There will also be days where the depression takes hold and I cannot and will not think of anything but her. Grief ebbs and flows through our bodies, through our lives, through every day living.

There is no timeline and you do not have to be okay.

Crying in Target

My family's compound losses caused significant financial strain on my husband and me. Between the time off work, the travel expenses to see his family, the ER vet bill, and already living paycheck to paycheck, it forced my hand to do gig work every weekend.

My gig work of choice became Target same day delivery. I started as early as December 18th, just eight days after her passing, and continued weekly for over a year. Going into Target was always a fun time for me, but as the seasons changed and I experienced all the firsts I talked about before, I found myself constantly crying in Target.

As the items in the dollar spot changed from Christmas, to Valentine's Day and the clothes changed from winter to spring to summer clothing, it broke me. In addition to needing headphones in at all times, I also needed sunglasses, so I could easily mask the crying. I tried with all my might to hold it in and let it all go as soon as I returned to my car, but sometimes the urges were too overwhelming.

During Christmas 2024, I would not accept any orders that required me to shop the seasonal aisles out of fear of a complete meltdown. How has it already been a year? How am I still stuck in a time that has long since passed? Will I ever move forward?

Doing gig work out of necessity was a constant reminder of what I lost. On the days I was so exhausted and depressed I could collapse, we still needed food, and rent was still due. The world did not stop just because mine did. On these days I cried over every trigger. A dog barking when I delivered the owner's groceries or walking past a Lamb Chop toy. One time I treated myself to an oat milk vanilla latte at the in-store Starbucks, but since I was so anxious, when I tried to put the cup into the cart I completely missed. Latte all over the floor, and I knew I could not afford another one. I could hardly afford that one. I stopped right there in the toy aisle and sobbed. How was this my life?

Eventually I became used to the triggers in the stores. I knew when to expect them. I could better manage my emotions. I would cry in the car or completely compartmentalize the job I was doing versus the emotions I felt. Now I can shop the seasonal aisles. I can go to Target for leisure. But I still get the feeling in the pit of my stomach.

The time is passing and she is still not here and some days I still cry in Target.

In life and death, you always stole my heart

When we walked in the door, collar in hand, I plopped down on the couch, asked for my girl's favorite Lamb Chop toy, pointed at the TV, and said "Bayside." My husband knew exactly what I was talking about. It was the YouTube video from my favorite Bayside show of all time, where you can see me front and center, having the absolute time of my life. This is my emotional support video because it reminds me of what happiness feels like. In the past, my worst days could be brightened by watching this video. Not this night.

I couldn't channel the happiness that night, but I still leaned on my favorite band. For months I listened to them as I slept. Every moment of every day I had to be awake, Anthony Raneri's voice played in my ears. I couldn't walk

Kekoa or be out in public unless I brought Bayside with me.

So when I incorporated Bayside into my monthly ritual, it just made sense. On the one month anniversary of her death, I watched a video my husband took of her final moments. That night as he recorded it seemed so weird, but I have never been more thankful for his ability to foresee exactly what I would need. What did I say? Did I tell her everything I needed to? What time was it? The timestamp on the video was 9:07. Her heart stopped beating 1:04 into the video recording. 9:08 PM.

On the second month anniversary, I decided at 9:07 PM on the 10th, Kekoa and I would set out on a walk and listen to "Winter" by Bayside. "Winter" was written after the band was in a car accident resulting in the loss of their drummer, John "Beatz" Holohan.

Every month to this day, we take our 9:08 walks and we listen to "Winter." It's our ritual.

This isn't the only way I incorporated Bayside. Their first show after her loss was in April and I felt immense guilt over leaving Kekoa and the "what if's" wouldn't stop plaguing me. The night Pueo died, I was supposed to be in New York City seeing Ariana Madix on her book tour, but the show was canceled because she got COVID. Bayside was the first event I was going to attend since that night.

I sat in Pueo's bed, held her collar and talked to her. For a moment it felt like she was standing right in front of me saying "mama, why are you crying in my bed. It's Bayside day. You never spend this much time with us on Bayside day, and that's okay because Bayside day is for you."

When I saw them live in April and May of 2024, I soaked in every moment. I enjoyed time with friends and cried after every single show. I allowed myself to feel joy in the way my broken heart could.

In October, I decided to embark on a spiritual journey to the desert. Bayside was playing at Pappy & Harriet's in Pioneertown, California. I bought a ticket to the show without the slightest idea on how I would make this crazy idea happen. Then, I bought a plane ticket, booked an Airbnb, and found a Bayside friend online to drive me around all weekend.

I landed in Los Angeles around 10 am and took an Uber to Forest Lawn Memorial Park - Hollywood Hills, where Bob Barker and Matthew Perry are both buried. Their deaths were two celebrity deaths that really affected me. Matthew Perry's grave marker was not there yet, but there were flowers marking his space. Then I found Bob, sat on the ground next to him and sobbed. In that moment I grieved for people I did not know, but it was all the same grief just coming to the surface. Grief doesn't differentiate between personal and distant loss once the door is open.

After what felt like the perfect start to the trip, I took another Uber to Hollywood Boulevard. I saw the Hollywood Walk of Fame, got VanLeeuwen ice cream and some coffee, and waited for my friend to pick me up. We did a short *Vanderpump Rules* tour, seeing some of the restaurants owned by various cast members, and got sandwiches at Something About Her. Then we started our trek out to the desert.

The next day was Bayside day. We did a little sightseeing in Joshua Tree, went to a crystal shop, got coffee, and headed to Pioneertown. In the town there was no cell service. I had to connect to a satellite to even send a text message. The town provided me a true opportunity to disconnect from the outside world. In the town, there was a little market and one vendor was doing permanent bracelets. I always wanted one, and this seemed like the perfect time. I decided on a purple chain since Pueo was my purple girl, always sporting a purple harness and leash. I chose a moon with a star for the charm, since she was my sun, moon and stars, truly my everything. Every time I look at this bracelet, I think of her and our permanent connection.

I kissed the mayor, Sam the goat. Not the greatest of all time, an actual goat. We got tacos and we waited for the show. A very typical Bayside day.

When the time came for them to perform, I looked to the sky and took in the stars, the moon, the crisp October evening, and watched my favorite band perform. I cannot explain it, but that show changed me. The trip to California changed the trajectory of my grief. After the trip, I felt lighter, calmer, centered. It was a perfect trip.

Bayside has been a part of me since their music saved my life in 2012. They saved me again in 2024. When I lose Kekoa, they'll save me again. And again. And again.

Whoever your Bayside is, let the music take you over. Let the music heal you. Let the music help you to live again. Cry to it, sing to it, scream your lungs out to it, dance to it, smile to it.

Bayside is a cult. A cult that saved me.

Kekoa: Strength

keh-koh-ah

Finding grounding in grief and power in presence

A Love Letter to Kekoa

On the one year anniversary of Pueo's passing, I wrote this to Kekoa:

Koa,

When thinking about you and Pueo, I always swore you would leave us before her. She always had a perfect bill of health, and you're my IBS king. Although I wish it could have stayed the four of us together, in hindsight, I'm glad you are here with me. You have been the perfect dog to grieve with. My comfort and my rock. You became my best friend and stepped up right away in her absence. In some ways you came out of your shell, since she was so demanding. You've become a wonderful big brother, something we never thought you'd be. Although you and Lucy are still finding your groove, sharing your time with mom, and figuring out your space, you've adapted so seamlessly.

My boy, I don't think I would be here to write these words without you. I don't know that I would have survived. I don't know that I would have pushed myself to do the hard things. You made me better, and you are still making me better. Everything I do is for you.

Surviving Dog Syndrome

I'm sure that's not the name for it, but it feels like a syndrome to me.

Kekoa and Pueo grew up together. She was born in 2015 and he was born in 2017. As they aged together, they became closer and were such a perfect pair. Koa is sweet and soft, a cuddly little bear. He enjoys bedtime with his mom, playing ball, long walks, and is laid back.

Pueo was... the opposite. She was our fierce protector. She only cuddled on her own time and she was always on guard dog duty. She took her job very seriously and it's why her nickname was the poo poo police. Everything we did was on her time and her time only. There was no peace when she wanted something. Pueo kept our household in check and always on our best behavior.

Growing up, she was in perfect health. The only time she saw the inside of the vet's office was for her annual shots and check ups, the occasional tummy issue or the time she ate a bee.

Koa on the other hand, from age two had a benign cyst on his back that randomly burst open one day. He's the king of irritable bowel syndrome (IBS), and picked up every disease known to dog at the dog park. He was my problem child. Thinking about them aging I always assumed Pueo would live well into her teens, since her mother passed at 16 years old, and we would lose Kekoa early.

If I'm being honest, this scenario sounded easier to me. I'd lose Koa and that would teach me how to cope when we lost her. But that's just not how it happened.

Instead, we lost Pueo when she was only eight years old. The dog with perfect health collapsed in front of my eyes, and four hours later she was gone.

Unfortunately, because of the suddenness of her death, Koa did not get to say goodbye, but I do believe he knew she was sick. He knew when we left that night, that he wouldn't see her again. She was silently training him on how to take over her responsibilities.

As the months progressed, Koa didn't actively grieve as I thought he might. They were attached to each other, and I thought surely I would have to manage my own grief along with his. In reality he knew his duty was to help me manage. Help me get out of bed every day. Help me grieve this massive loss.

Now, Koa and I are closer than ever. As time goes on, I am seeing signs of his aging. He will be eight years old in just four short weeks. The anxiety is settling in on this reality. Every little thing he does I am convinced that he is dying. Every fatty lump, every little cough, every weird poop. I have closely examined more poop in the last 18 months than I ever thought I would. He is always fine, but losing her suddenly to hemangiosarcoma traumatized me.

In the weeks leading up to her death, she was being fussier than ever about eating and she was walking slower on late night walks. I called the vet and they said as long as she's eating, she's fine and we chalked the slower walks up to aging. If I had trusted my gut, we would have at least had some advance notice, but as I said in *Grief is Grief and Hard is Hard*, grieving her was always going to seem impossible.

These days my gut is always wrong. I am always convinced something is off, everything is cancer, everything is going to take my boy from me. And that's the surviving dog syndrome, the fear and anxiety of your surviving dog meeting the same fate as the dog you're grieving. He will soon be eight and I need to allow myself to know that's okay.

In retrospect, there would never be an easier dog to lose. How can losing someone you love with your entire being be "easier" than the other? Had we lost Koa first like I theorized for years, I think Pueo would have grieved hard. She would cry and pace any time I took him anywhere without her. I think her and I would've been crying together. But now Kekoa is the dog who helped me grieve my soulmate and through our shared experience, has become my heart dog.

So as I go through this surviving dog syndrome, I am actively cherishing every day I have with my two healthy dogs. I will continue routine vet check ups, but I will also continue to check every symptom and I will trust my gut if anything seems off. Maybe one day I will rid myself of this syndrome, but maybe not. Maybe I will be hypervigilant about my dogs for the rest of my life.

Like everything else with grief, things change over time. Things evolve and we just have to let grief run its course, no matter how long it takes.

***

Since the original writing, I took Kekoa to the vet for his annual check up and vaccinations. At that appointment, to ease my anxiety, we conducted a senior bloodwork panel and all tests came back perfectly healthy and normal. I would simultaneously like time to slow down, but I also want him to be nine. I need the anxiety of him facing the same fate to lessen. To believe that I will have more time with him and this time I will not feel cheated. I am not sure if I will feel that once he turns nine and I am not sure what this syndrome has in store for me, but I do know I am grateful that as of today, he is a healthy and happy boy.

Finding your safe space

When Pueo died, I hoped everyone would be in my corner. Knowing me is knowing the depth of my love for Pueo. My inner circle knew that she was not just a dog to me. She was everything.

So when I heard comments like:

"Well what about your work?"

"You've made everything about you these last few months."

"You have to want it to get better, and right now it seems like you don't."

I had to re-evaluate everything, everyone, every relationship, including my mom, my stepdad, my husband. I had to work through it all in therapy. My therapist always said

I had to accept everyone as they are and stop having expectations of people they would never meet.

It was a difficult process. One that made me face hard truths about people who have been in my life for years and people I have to be around and talk to daily.

I decided I wouldn't have expectations of understanding from people who couldn't comprehend the human/animal connection. I couldn't have expectations of emotional depth from people who have not explored their own emotions. I couldn't have expectations of grace from people who were unwilling to offer it. I could not have expectations of a safe environment with people I have seen take others' tragedies and turn them into jokes.

I adjusted. I accepted people for who they were, their lived experiences, and my lived experience with them. I decided that deep conversations weren't worth it with some and surface-level friendship wasn't worth it with others.

I shifted my time and energy from people who no longer aligned with who I wanted to be in light of Pueo's death onto people who were willing to do the work with me. People who were willing to listen to me and repeatedly tell me "I know this sucks" no matter if they'd needed to say it 100 times that week.

I opened myself up to new friendships and I reopened myself to my family little by little as it felt comfortable. I started writing, reading and doing the work so I could talk to myself and treat myself like a friend. I poured countless hours into Lucy and Kekoa.

These adjustments did not happen overnight. It took about 9 months to accept, shift, and shape, but I got there. Inevitably, I will lose Kekoa. I will lose Lucy. I will lose other pets and humans and the grief will be heavy for me again. But this time, I will know who I can trust, who I can go to and who has my back unconditionally, and judgment-free.

Find your safe space.

Find your peace.

Setting boundaries

Along with safe spaces, it is very important to set boundaries. When I wrote about the firsts, I mentioned that I put a full stop on holidays for a year and told my family this was my boundary. When everyone inevitably crossed this boundary, I was furious. Every time someone mentioned Halloween or Christmas, I was furious. Why are we even discussing this when I said no? Why was this so hard to understand?

I learned the hard way that my boundary should also have considered the needs of my husband. He wanted normalcy, and I felt normalcy was a complete betrayal. How could anything be normal without her? How could life move forward? In hindsight, we should have discussed our needs and found a compromise, but I was not willing to listen. Everything had to be how I wanted it to be, and everyone knew it was best to fall in line with me. It wasn't fair. At this point, I am not sure what the compromise could have been. What I do know is I hurt my loved ones, especially the one who loves her like I do.

I placed all of Pueo's toys in bins and set them next to the bookshelf I created for her and her belongings. For over a year now, my husband has asked if we could move them or create space for something else, and I have said no.

I took the 10th of the month each month to honor and grieve her, no matter what that meant for work. I needed the time, and I was not going to budge.

I never allowed myself to shrink or minimize my grief. Sometimes this may have made people uncomfortable, but I would not allow anyone to make me feel uncomfortable about my pain. "How are you?" was met with honesty. I cried when I needed to cry, no matter where I was. I was always open, honest, and vulnerable. I talked about her all the time and still do, as if she was still here with me.

Set the boundaries and never shrink yourself down for the comfort of others. I would give this advice about almost any situation in life, but especially in your grief. Just make sure the boundaries make sense for you and for those who are also deeply affected by the loss.

The things we cannot do...yet

Every month I attend the Anti-Cruelty Society support group and at this point, I am one of the veterans. Many people coming in are very fresh in their grief. A week, two, maybe a month. Every session people ask if it's okay that they can't _____. Fill in the blank with things like, pick up their pets toys, clean up their water bowl, move their bed, etc. Some people sleep with their pets' ashes, and some with collars. I sleep with her lamby. Everyone is doing what feels right to them, while simultaneously feeling like it is wrong.

Dozens of times, I have reassured people that this is okay, and this is normal, because it is. For me, I thought I had done all the things aside from moving from our apartment, which will happen one day.

I moved the food bowls, I put away the toys, I moved her bed, I washed the blankets. Everything in the apartment was cleaned up and in its chosen spot. I thought I was done.

That was until I realized I was going to have people in the back seat of my SUV.

The night she died, I knew something was wrong when we got in the car and she didn't make a sound. Not a single sound. Pueo had always been a terror in the car. She would cry louder than the stereo could ever go. I would've given anything to hear her cry that night, or any day after.

When we got to the animal hospital, they helped her out of the car and onto a gurney. The photos of me petting her and waiting for them haunt me. I've felt immense guilt about not being with her during her final hour. She hated the vet and she hated being away from me, but they would not allow me to go in the back of the hospital with her. The back seat of my SUV was the last place of mine where she existed. The last place I saw her before I knew I was losing her.

For months, I couldn't bring myself to drive the SUV. The towel that my husband carried her to the car in sat in the same spot in the backseat for months. Eventually, I had the towel turned into a teddy bear, and it is perfect. Eventually I let Kekoa and Lucy go in the backseat.

But never a human.

So when the situation arose that I may have to pass this hurdle, I panicked. I cried for two days and eventually I had to just accept the fate. I had to use my SUV and I had to let someone sit back there. Over a year before, this same situation occurred and I just absolutely could not let it happen. No. But this time I could be *sort of* ready.

So I got in the car, I repeated aloud to myself that I was not erasing her, that it was still her spot and that this was okay. I unbuckled her seatbelt and placed it on the seat. I cried, and cried as I drove to pick up my passenger.

When I got to the moment someone would have to sit there, I was paralyzed, but I was also wrong. Never in my life had I been so happy to be wrong. Only one person needed to be in the back seat, instead of two as I originally thought. I asked them to sit on the other side, and of course they did without question. Pueo's spot behind the driver's seat was still hers.

I wasn't ready and I'm still not ready. The back seat may always be like the empty spot at the table, like the toys on the floor, like the empty bed and you know what? That's okay.

Be kind to yourself. Your timeline is your timeline.

We can do hard things

That has been my motto since February 10, 2024. On that day, Koa and I set out on a five and a half mile hike. I had never truly hiked before. Walking trails? Sure. Have I ever enjoyed it? Absolutely not. But this was different.

Losing her is the hardest thing I have ever had to live through and at that time, I did not think I could actually do it. I wanted to leave earth to be with her so many times. How could I carry on life without her?

So that day we headed to a trail that is no more than five minutes away from me. It is a trail that I drive past every day on my way to work. According to AllTrails, we hiked 5.3 miles in two hours and fifty minutes, burning 1,566 calories. The trail was full of hills, mud, and rocky terrain.

It was well out of my comfort zone. There were times I wanted to give up on the trail, but I couldn't, especially not when we were too far in to turn around. There were no shortcuts back and we were in the middle of nowhere. It was the first time in two months I did not need to have Bayside playing in my ears to feel safe and calm.

As we trekked up hills, through mud, to waterfalls, we felt her. Wherever we were, she was. I have photos of Kekoa looking into the sky as if he was looking for her. We did it. We did something that two years ago I would have never done, but that day I set out to prove to myself, Briar, *you can do hard things.*

Hard things have not always been hikes. Sometimes it has been merely surviving. One time it was Lucy's graduation from puppy training. One time I actually worked, granted it was a work from home day, but I still did it. One month it was saying enough is enough when it came to Lucy's training and feeling like she was being bullied by the other dog moms. I pulled her from class that day and started doing individual sessions. This month the hard thing was having a good day. It seems simple and easy, right? It hasn't been. This month Kekoa and I went on our first run in over a year. Lucy and I spent the afternoon training at Petsmart. Being with Koa is hard. Going for runs is hard. Having Lucy is hard. Everything is a reminder of what I lost, what I've gained and what I've had to endure.

So every month I do the hard things because we can and because we have to. Losing your animal companion is the hardest thing many of us will experience. But we can do it. We can do the hard things.

I'm so happy I could die

The joy sits heavy in my chest, as if pneumonia is creeping in. It sits in the same place where sadness has lived for 436 days. When I first felt this just a few days ago, I was confused. Why was I so uncomfortable? Am I getting sick? Why did the laughter and the smile hurt?

It then dawned on me that it has been over 400 days since I felt *pure* joy. All of my joy has come through forced smiles, a broken heart, sad eyes, and just enough fake energy to maybe convince others that I could be happy. But I couldn't.

Realizing that I had started to feel pure joy again while playing with Kekoa and Lucy came with a flurry of con-fusion. The first thing that came to mind was a song on

Bayside's recent album *There Are Worse Things Than Being Alive.* There is a song that shares the title of this post. A song that captures the contradiction I couldn't yet put into words: feeling euphoric and devastated at the same time. Being so happy it's almost unbearable, and still so sad it hurts to breathe.

There are days I am truly so happy I could die. We have rebuilt our cute little life, even through the void of losing Pueo. Kekoa has become my right hand man, my confidant, and my teddy bear. We adopted Lucy 6 months after losing Pueo and although the road was difficult, I love her energy, her affection and I love that she is ours.

But every day, I am so sad I want to cry. I miss my old life. I miss Pueo, I miss pure joy. I miss her quirks, her energy, and I miss feeling complete. I miss just feeling happy or just feeling sad. No strange and uncomfortable in-betweens.

Every day, grief is a new journey. It's like riding a roller coaster with a blindfold on. Constant highs and lows that must be accepted and ventured into. You have to learn that happy and sad are not simple, straightforward emotions. They are complex and they can live within one another. It took 436 days to feel real happiness again. Even if the moments are fleeting, they can exist again after loss. The happiness may never feel the same, it may feel heavier and it may still feel like something is missing, because it is. But you can become so happy you feel like you could overdose on dopamine.

Daily Tasks without them

You do not realize just how intertwined they are with every-thing you do until they are gone. Every routine is structured around them. Their eating, walking, playing, and snack times are woven into our lives. More than that, they are always there.

Pueo was a velcro dog, never leaving my side for a second. She reminded me of what people with human children experience, because she had no boundaries whatsoever. So when I tried to lift weights or get back on the Peloton, I simply could not. I realized that she was always next to me, sometimes intrusively, when I was lifting. She was always nearly getting hit by pedals when I was cycling.

Because she barked and wanted to greet every dog and human she saw on walks, we took certain paths at certain times to keep her calm. When Kekoa and I went to bed, she and my husband would have special daddy and daughter playtime or take special extra walks together.

She demanded attention. She kept us on our toes, never really knowing what she would want next. So when that was gone, everything felt empty. Different.

To this day, my husband still feels the grief over walking the dogs and he constantly asks when I think is a good time to walk them so there are less people. I have to gently remind him that it is much less of an issue now that she is gone. Kekoa and Lucy are calmer walkers. For over a year, he avoided staying up late because he lost his nighttime buddy. Lucy has started to fill that void for him.

For me, I had to change our feeding and snack routine for a few months and I did not get back to consistent exercise for well over a year. I would start and stop repeatedly, always missing my shadow. The best workout buddy I could have asked for. Lucy has started to fill this void for me.

Eventually life adapts to their absence. Our routines change, and day to day life starts to feel less empty or lonely. We fill voids with different things. That could be friends, family, or another animal companion. I have met people who have used the loss of their animal companion to provide them with more freedom to travel or hang out with friends. I adopted Lucy. No matter what path you decide to take, the tides will turn. One day you will adapt to a life that feels normal again.

Eternal, present love

'I loved them' is a common phrase among grievers. Society treats grief as if it exists only in 'before' and 'after.' They lived, they died.

Sure, Pueo lived in the past tense, but my love for her remains as present as it has ever been. Love and grief go hand in hand as one does not exist without the other. To love is to grieve, whether that grief is a friendship ending or the death of a loved one. We feel grief before the death even happens. This has been named anticipatory grief.

We can continue to honor them and carry them with us by speaking of our love in the present tense. Today. I love her today, I will love her tomorrow and I will never, ever love her in the past tense.

Lucy: Resilience

loo-see

The wild way forward. Growing through chaos and loving through change

A Love Letter to Lucy

On the one year anniversary of Pueo's passing, I wrote this to Lucy:

Lucy,

I tell you all the time, I'm sad you're here because my girl is gone, but I am also so glad you're here. You being in our lives means my girl is gone, but it also means we get to love you for the rest of your life. You never met Pueo, but I see her in you every day. I know she sent you to us at exactly the right time.

You were given the difficult task of filling the empty space left in our home and hearts when we lost our girl. You and Koa were meant to help heal me and sew together my shattered heart. You were brought to us to show us it's okay to open up and love again.

It's been a long road, and you have tested my patience to no end, but it's all been worth it. We are going through the same Petsmart training classes as Pueo and I did and you graduated puppy class yesterday, December 9th. The date is not a coincidence. It's a sign you were meant for us. We were meant for you. This is your forever home. Lucy is your final name, and we love you forever.

Everything Wrapped Into One

Today is Tuesday, June 10th, 2025. I lost Pueo 18 months ago, and for the first year, I told myself I would take off of work every month on the 10th to do hard things. At least until January 10, 2025.

Well, that wasn't the case. January came around and it still felt too hard. Now, I am an advocate of doing hard things, especially in the face of the hardest thing I have ever done. But this was too much. In March I worked from home and had a mental breakdown in a meeting. So I took April off. I couldn't do it. I was not ready.

In April when I told my friends that I was taking off, they said... okay... I support you, but... when is this going to end?

I knew it came from a place of love, and if I said I would be doing this until the end of time, I would've been met with support. I told them I just was not ready yet. It was never the plan to do this longer than a year, but my grief wanted what it wanted.

May was a Saturday, so that had no extra complications.

But today is Tuesday. It's not my work from home day, it is just plain old Tuesday. My original plan was to switch my work from home day, but something came up. My options were to push off an important meeting for another few weeks, or embrace the hard thing. Little did I know, today I would meet our new boss and make an unforeseen connection with him.

He came into my office to learn about my work journey and to get to know me as a person. Anyone who walks into my office can't help but notice the photo collage on my wall. It includes everyone important in my life, but mostly my dogs. He tells me about his transition and how he loves my photos, but is not sure that his office space is permanent so he has yet to decorate. I replied, "I always have to have my dogs on my computer." He said he likes to have his kids and his dog, who passed away a few months prior.

When he mentioned his dogs passing, I could tell there was a shift in him, like maybe he should not have said anything, but I responded with our story. It turns out his dog passed the same way as Pueo. There one moment, gone the next. He opened up about when he and his wife adopted her, recalling seeing puppies wheeled into a rescue and knowing they needed this specific dog. He lit up. I gave him the space to talk about her, and he lit up.

So as I sit here at my desk, thinking about my girl. Thinking about that day, thinking about how much time has passed and how little time has passed at the same time, thinking about days where I couldn't leave bed on the 10th, I have no choice but to be proud of myself. I've come out of my darkest depression and opted to make the best of a truly heartbreaking experience. I've decided to make today both a first and a hard thing, all wrapped into one.

I've learned. I've grown. I've overcome. I've provided safe spaces. I've done hard things. I've made myself proud.

And I hope I've made her proud.

Adoption Journey

We brought Lucy home June 22, 2024, a little over six months since losing Pueo.

On June 20, I saw her photos online and told myself I would meet her the next day. I did not tell anyone I was going. It was not until I was at the shelter waiting to be brought back to see her that I told my friends. I did not want any outside influence, or doubt, nothing. I just wanted to meet a dog and see how it felt. I told myself I wouldn't adopt unless it felt RIGHT.

So on June 21, when I went in and said I wanted to meet Mary Puppins, they asked "Are there any other dogs you would like to meet?" I said no. It was her or no one. I felt the fluttering in my chest like I was about to meet the dog who would change me, and I was right.

I went into the room and patiently waited while they brought her in and as soon as she ran in, I started to cry. I loved her. Instantly.

She was the cutest, sweetest, and craziest little girl. She was the challenge I was looking for, the crazy girl energy I yearned for.

I texted my friends and said "ummmm... I am at the shelter and I am fucked."

It really did not help that she had white mittens on her back feet with little freckles like Pueo, and the tip of her tail was white like Pueo. If I had the final say, she would have come home with me that day. But there were two issues:

1. She was heartworm positive. I had no idea what that meant, what that meant for the longevity of her life, nothing. I just knew I could not risk the same heartbreak over again if I could help it.

2. The boys had to meet her and I knew my husband was not ready.

So I went home and we discussed and my husband agreed to bring Kekoa to meet her the next day. I did my research and learned that heartworm would not affect her long-term health so long as we followed the treatment protocol. All night I thought about her, and I had to be at the shelter as soon as they opened. I needed her. No one else could have my dog.

It was a short meeting since it was nearly 100 degrees that day and full of tension. My husband was not happy with this decision, Kekoa was confused and overstimulated, but ultimately, they agreed to let me take her home.

The first few months were not easy. Learning Lucy's habits and triggers resulted in two minor injuries.

We thought we had to rehome her. We had to keep her calm through her treatment, she was medicated, untrained, younger than we expected and overall more challenging than expected. To manage, she was given her kennel as her space. They were fed in different rooms, always separated for treats. Then once heartworm treatment was over and the medication wore off, she was able to run around and expel all of her excess energy. A few months later, we started training at Petsmart and now she is an American Kennel Club Canine Good Citizen.

Moving through it was hard and my boys were miserable. They were not ready for what felt like moving on. Over the past year, we have all grown and adapted. Through a lot of trial and error, grief, healing, crying, frustration, and fleeting happiness, here we are. Lucy is our Stitch, and we wouldn't trade this past year for anything (unless science could bring Pueo back to us, of course).

Here are my top lessons from the past year of adopting through grief and after the loss of my soulmate:

> 1. You can never replace them. Adopting Lucy did not replace Pueo. Not even close. I love Lucy with

every piece of me and she had big shoes to fill, but there will always be a void in my heart for Pueo. I will never stop missing her and nothing can ever stop that. Lucy did not replace the void, Lucy made my heart grow.

2. The 3/3/3 theory is true... to an extent. The first three days are an initial adjustment period. They may be overwhelmed or unsure. After three weeks, the dog should start to settle into routines, learn what is expected, and start to show their personalities. After three months, the family should be adjusted, and confident, but every dog is different. It has taken Koa almost the full year to warm up to Lucy. While I may never know why, I believe Kekoa was still grieving, and Lucy's energy was too much for him at first. Now that she is a little older and calmer, he has accepted his new sibling.

3. You can do it. After two days, I swore I could not do it. It was too much work, too difficult, I did not have the patience. The truth was, my anxiety was lying to me. I could do it. You can do it.

4. Grief and love don't only co-exist, they are the same thing. Healing is not linear and joy can return.

5. You can overcome. We thought we could not

overcome the issues between Lucy and Koa, but through adaptations inside and outside, and months of training, they have very few, if any, issues. Patience and persistence are your friend.

6. You cannot force your healing, your readiness, or your timeline to adopt on the others in your family. My husband and I agreed when I adopted Lucy that she was mine. He was not ready and did not want the responsibility. He would help with walks or things when I needed him to, but she was mine. He came around to her in his own time and there was nothing I could have done or should have done to speed it up. In hindsight, adopting her was not the right thing for my family at the time, but she healed me. I needed her and she needed us. Of course since my husband did not want her, all she wanted was him and now they are glued together and have a beautiful relationship.

7. You don't get the dog you want, you get the dog you need. Lucy has been the perfect dog and one of the two major turning points in my grief. She helped me heal in ways I otherwise would not have. She was exactly what I needed and I believe Pueo sent her to me. Thanks, poo girl.

Overall, there is no right time to adopt. Some adopt after weeks, some months, some years, some never again. Only you can know when the time is right and if you can accept another dog into your life. I know my soul dog sent me Lucy. She knew exactly what I needed, but that is my journey.

Just remember, you can do it. The work is all worth it.

When Should I Adopt Again?

Our house had the perfect balance. Two girls, two boys. Two humans, two dogs. When she died, I became the lone girl. The energy shifted. Before I even considered adopting again, I found a graphic with key questions. It became my guide and a checkpoint to determine whether I was truly ready.

Am I ready for a huge change in routine? No.

Do I have hesitation or anxiety about a new animal? Yes.

Do I feel I have fully processed my loss? No.

Do I feel I don't "deserve" a new animal? No.

What problems do I have that I believe a new animal will help? Loneliness.

Have I created new outlets for coping and comfort? No.

Am I adopting to "quit" grieving? No.

Has my grief anger subsided? No.

I use this graphic often now in my support circles to help people navigate the challenge of deciding when it's the right time.

For me, the most important piece was anger. My anger persisted for many, many months so I knew it was not the time to adopt. After a few months, I began browsing again out of curiosity. I stopped at an animal shelter and played with a couple dogs that just didn't feel right. I left feeling guilty. Feeling like I should not have been there.

Then I was on Facebook one night and found a dog named Leo. Leo was a black and white heeler mix, a dog my husband always wanted. He had features like Pueo. He was black and white with freckles. He seemed perfect. I scheduled a time to meet with the person rehoming him, but the night before, I couldn't sleep. I had paralyzing anxiety and I cancelled. She told me Leo would be at a local shelter called St. Hubert's.

Every few weeks I would casually browse their website and just see what girl dogs they had available and nothing caught my eye... until her. Mary Puppins. A beautiful "lab mix" with the perfect amount of derp and features that reminded me just of Pueo. I had to meet her.

After the boys and I met her, she came home on a 10-day trial. On the first night, I had a meltdown. I couldn't do this. Thoughts ran through my head, and fear paralyzed me. I second guessed all of it, would Kekoa adapt? Would Andrew accept her? Was I ready for the routine change, the responsibility? She had heartworm disease when we adopted her, would that affect her long term health? Could I manage the treatment? Everything ran through my head and paralyzed me with fear.

But I could do it. I can do hard things. I kept saying, we will only keep her if it works and everyone in my life said "you're keeping that dog, why pretend like you won't."

They were right.

Every journey is different. I've met people who adopted immediately and it worked out and I've met people who could never adopt again and it worked out. The question, "When should I adopt again?" is so deeply personal. There is no right answer. There is no wrong answer. I based my decision on the questions I found, my heart, and what my gut told me.

The answer is simple: it has to feel right. Lucy felt right.

What are you doing to honor your animal companion?

This question is always posed to my monthly support group. Some people have expressed their love and grief through art or gardening or physical items. Some have used a journal, some *wink* have started a blog to help others. There are thousands of ways to express ourselves, to express our grief and honor our animal companions.

All of the shops and services I have used are in the *Grief Resources* chapter. My first order of business was to purchase what was offered through the crematorium. Since we did not have much time to think or prepare, we purchased card stock and ink prints of her nose and paw prints, along with a cremation ring from Ken's Cremation Creations.

Then I took to Etsy to find memorial pieces. These included keychains for my husband and I, new wedding bands with her name engraved and a necklace with her face that I still wear every day.

Once I found these physical pieces, I bought waterproof, airtight bins. They hold her blanket, her most loved lamb chop, and the hoodie I was wearing the night she died. These containers were from Target and have helped in preserving her scent. I am so thankful. Then I decided she deserved her own space for her belongings, photos, and urn. Target came to my rescue again. I purchased a cube shelf, filling it with photos, her favorite toys, bandanas, collars, and other keepsakes. That area now also contains a family rocking chair that belonged to my late great grandmother.

Bayside, my favorite band, also became part of my grief ritual. For weeks, all I listened to was Bayside. I could not fall asleep without them, I couldn't walk Kekoa without them, I was not doing much of anything without their music playing. So on the 10th of every month, I listen to their song "Winter", a song about losing their best friend and band mate in a fatal car crash. I start the song at 9:06 pm, which is when the doctor told us she was passing, 9:07 pm was when they administered euthanasia and by 9:08 pm she was gone. On nice nights, Kekoa and I walk to the place where Pueo and I would run in the morning. On cold or rainy nights, I will sit with Kekoa in Pueo's bed, which has now become his.

I've had three tattoos done in the last year.

I honor her every day. I talk about her, write about her, cry about her. I never diminish my grief. I find joy in the uncomfortable conversations, the ones that push people to think of grief differently. I try to provide safe spaces for others to open up and talk about their loved ones. I work to destigmatize grief, especially pet loss grief, and this is a tall task. Grief is something everyone experiences, yet it's completely taboo to talk about openly. People experience loss every day, yet society has pushed us all into support groups and made us feel like discussing our loss is too much or somehow wrong.

I honor her every single day and I plan to for the rest of my life.

Think about what feels meaningful to you. Whether it's a tattoo, a ritual, a dedicated space, or just talking about them. Honor your companion in a way that speaks to your heart.

Learning to Live Again

I had absolutely no idea how to handle grief and this deep, all consuming sadness. I have lost before. Friends, family members, but never anyone as deep rooted in me and in my life as Pueo. I had to learn all new coping mechanisms. This is a list of methods that helped me and other methods I heard through support group.

1. Therapy - If you are going through anticipatory grief and do not have a therapist, please secure one now. If you have already lost your pet, seek out a therapist who specializes in grief. Some therapists specialize in pet loss specifically, though they may be harder to find. I am a huge advocate for therapy in general, but having someone to talk to during

grief is extremely important. You may begin to feel like you have exhausted your friends or your family (you likely have not), but your therapist is someone you can rely on to listen. After a while, therapy can feel like you are reopening the wound. I encourage you to be mindful of this and make sure therapy is helping your mental health. Take a break if you need to, that is okay.

2. Support groups - I have a list of support groups in the grief resources chapter. Use them as often as you need. The Association for Pet Loss and Bereavement chat room is open almost daily. I added the times to my calendar so I remembered when the space was available. The Anti-Cruelty Society group is the one I used the most and through it I have found friends and created a Discord channel to use in between meetings and stay connected with those who are living through similar experiences.

3. Coloring, art, drawing, knitting, anything crafty to keep you busy - Personally, I am not creative in those ways, but I did really enjoy coloring and many days it was the only way I survived my time at home. It allowed me to watch television without letting my brain wander. My brain was focused on the TV and coloring between the lines which kept

my anxiety in check. I have met people who just needed to keep their hands busy with knitting and crocheting and I have friends who created paintings and pillows. This helped them process grief by drawing their pet or scenes that reminded them of their pet.

4. Music - I have talked at length about the music. I let it guide me, never taking my headphones off. It provided a real distraction for my mind. If I was singing the songs, my mind could not wander to the grief. Bayside was the only reason I could go to the grocery store without breaking down in tears or I could sit at my desk and actually get work done. Without the music, I could never have held it together when I had to.

5. Letting it out - On the note of keeping it together, also let it out. I cried in her bed so much, so often, so loudly that my neighbor asked me once if we got a small dog because she heard whimpering. Some people have found that setting aside time to grieve helped get them through the day. Knowing they could go home and grieve for a certain amount of time. Find whatever feels right for you to let it out. If you absorb one piece of advice from this, let it be to not bottle it up. Grief must be felt and if you do not actively let it out, it will come out. Possibly as

emotional outbursts, or even as physical reactions. Your body can make you sick if you do not let the grief out to breathe.

6. Set up a space for them, if it feels right - I struggled with this one. I couldn't decide where to place her ashes or what felt right for her belongings. Eventually I set up a bookshelf next to her bed and placed her, her collars, her favorite toys, photos of her and her bandanas on it. I placed her toys in airtight containers. Her bed and this corner became my safe space for a long time. I have heard of people making gardens as their safe space, but always do what feels best. If creating a specific space sounds painful to you, honor that.

7. Do what feels right - Ultimately, we all grieve differently and must do what feels right for ourselves. As I said in previous chapters, I had to work up the courage to make many changes. Moving her bed, washing her blankets, etc, but some people place all their pets belongings in a storage bin and never look back. What is right for me may not be right for you.

8. Re-establish or change routines - Waking up to her being gone, I could not fathom that I was only grabbing one treat from the bin, one bowl of food,

just one of everything. So my mom helped me change the routine. Instead of having a snack first thing in the morning, Kekoa would have breakfast, then his snack. Instead of our regular walking routes, we found new routes. Although I ended up falling into my old ones, I did so on my time.

9. Physical reminders - I still wear a necklace I had made after she died. I wear it every day along with the cremation ring. I put those on every morning. I also added a small stacking band to my wedding ring stack with her name on it. I got tattoos, I sleep with her lamby every night. These are daily reminders I can see or touch, keeping her close to me.

10. Honor them - By simply reading this book you are honoring them. Honor them in the way that feels right for you. Do what you believe they would want. Feel what you need to feel. Do things on your time since it is your journey and there is no timeline.

When They Still Speak

I was never a spiritual person. Growing up, I attended the Catholic Church, but I never felt part of the religion. It just never made sense to me. I believed you lived and you died and that was it. I have lost loved ones, but I never felt the need to see them again in the afterlife. The death of Pueo forced me to think differently.

I decided I could not live in a world where I would never see her again. I had to believe that she would be waiting for me on the other side because I could never accept that night as the final time.

Although I always struggled with my spiritual identity and if I even had one, I always believed in signs from the universe. Every time *Baba O'Riley* came on the radio, it was a sign from my friend Matt, who died tragically shortly after high school. If I heard Elvis or saw Betty Boop, I knew my great grandmom "Boot" was nearby.

For Pueo, I felt her everywhere, but I took to the geese. The geese became my number one indicator that she was around. Near my apartment, there is a pond where I used to sit with Pueo and Kekoa. After her death, Kekoa and I spent a lot of time there, and the geese often appeared. It seemed like they were always there when I needed them the most. They disappeared around the time we adopted Lucy. I'm sure this is a coincidence and is attributed to weather patterns, but I took this as a sign from Pueo that it was okay to have welcomed Lucy.

On New Year's Eve 2024, Kekoa and I were on a walk and I was devastated to be entering another year without her. It was supposed to be a short walk, but something in my body told me to go for a longer walk, so we went to the pond. On our walk, I was talking to her out loud and as we rounded the corner to the pond, I wished for geese, but I thought I was asking too much. After all, it had been six months without them. When we turned the corner, it was pitch black so I thought I had to be seeing things, but there they were. Two geese swimming in the pond.

Before my journey to California, I was very anxious, traumatized by the memory that I was not supposed to be home the night she died. If I was in California and something happened, I could not just get home. As I was walking

Kekoa that night and stressing over this thought, I heard geese overhead.

She showed up in dreams when I needed to see her, feel her, hold her, there she was. In these dreams she said "I am everywhere with you," in one she was panicking that she could not protect me and I had to release her from her duties. I said "it's okay, you can rest now." My fiercest protector was protecting me from the afterlife.

I have heard the shake of her collar, seen her head peeking around the corner for split seconds, and sometimes I felt like I could hear her talking to me.

I saw a medium, and although I would like to keep my reading private, I will share that she told me "Pueo said you always made promises and you never broke them." Now I hold myself to this with Kekoa and Lucy. If I make them a promise, I have to keep it. For them. For trust.

The back of this book is from the first dream I had of her. She was waiting for me in the woods, waiting to see me again. When I saw the medium, she also said this is where Pueo was waiting for me.

Grief and loss change us, changes our perspective on things and what we believe can be or is true. Although I still do not know what I believe, I know I will see her again. I know she will follow me, guide me, lead me and protect me until the day comes. They are always with us.

Tattoo Journey

At my core, I am a tattoo girlie. On my left arm, I have a Pueo owl. The Pueo owl is positioned so that when I am standing with my arms by my side, it faces backward. The placement was intentional because then she could watch my back forever. Immediately after she died, I thought I wanted a portrait of her on my right arm, opposite the Pueo owl, but my husband did not agree.

Now, normally, I am not one to listen to others about what I put on my body, but he asked one thing - that I wait a year and see if I change my mind. He was not ready to see her face on my body every day and I thought this was a valid request. I thought he would be wrong, and a year later I would be getting the tattoo, but he was not wrong.

One week after her passing, I had her nose tattooed on my left arm. It sits directly between my Bayside tattoo and the Pueo owl in a position where I can always see it, no matter the positioning of my arm. It also sits roughly at her height, on the arm that she laid on every night. It's perfect.

All year I thought about it. Pondering what I would do and one day it came to me. A bouquet of flowers to represent the birth and death months of every dog I have ever had. Posh, Snoopy, and Lucy were born in December, and Pueo died in December. Kekoa's birthday is in June, and Pueo's in August. A rose, poppy and holly. I had a friend from support group draw something up for me and we added lavender as it is a symbol of devotion. She was always devoted to me and I will always be devoted to her.

And so my tattoo was born. I waited the year and I had it done on January 10th, 2025. On the same day, I got my first hand tattoo. It is a very simple sun, moon and stars since I always told her I loved her more than the sun, the moon and all the stars in the sky. This tattoo also sits on my left arm, but on top of the hand that I hurt one time chasing her as she ran out of a Petco. I saw specialists, and no one has been able to figure out what it is so I just call it Pueoitis. Sometimes I will randomly have a flare up and I just think it is her saying hi and reminding me that she is here always.

Tattoos are a great way to honor your pet if that is something you are interested in. Take the time and think them through and the perfect idea will come to fruition.

Forgive Yourself

Through everything, the loss, the pain, the crying, the "stages," the rebuilding, the loss of self, the coping, the therapy, the memorials, we must reach a point of forgiving ourselves.

The guilt can still live there, but we cannot allow ourselves to live in a perpetual state of thinking that we did something wrong or that we could have done more. Trust me, if you could have done more, you would have done more. You made the best, most informed decisions you could make at the time, no matter the circumstance.

"Well, what if it was my fault?"

You still did your best.

Truthfully, I do not know if we ever fully release ourselves of guilt, but we can stop blaming ourselves or others.

When you feel the "I should have..." thoughts creeping in, remember what you did. Remember the life you gave them, the love they felt, how warm they felt in their bed, how they looked at you when you went for a long walk or played with their favorite toy. We cannot go back and change their death, and if we could, we all would. But we can go forward with forgiveness and grace for ourselves and for others.

Forgive yourself. You were the perfect parent for them. They lived a wonderful life. You did everything you could.

Identity, Rewritten

I have a photo of myself from two days before her passing and now I no longer recognize the girl in the photo. There is a twinkle in her eye, and a lightness that simply does not exist anymore.

I am no stranger to traumatic events, loss, and abandonment, but since these were part of my upbringing, they were just part of me. In the time before she died, I felt like my life was coming together. Sure, we were grieving and things were not necessarily easy, but I thought I had a great job, great friends, and best of all, a great little family unit.

We were figuring it all out.

I thought, "we just lost grandma and my husband and I are starting to find a flow again, everything is getting better, we are all healing," never did I think tragedy was around the corner. I was so naive.

In the weeks and months after her death, I was a disaster. I could hardly get myself together enough to work every day, but I had to. I cried every day for six months. I could not sleep without the help of medication. I could not stop talking about her or thinking about her, and everything showed on my face. It showed in the bags under my eyes and in my perpetual frown.

Even on my happiest of days, days spent going to see Bayside with my best friends, I could still see the puffiness in my eyes, and the loss of the twinkle.

Life handed me my most difficult hurdle so far and during the process, I lost myself.

Since losing her, I have become quieter, more anxious, more reserved. I have a harder time thinking for myself or thinking at all. Where I used to be able to laugh and joke and handle being teased, I cannot anymore. Losing her stripped me of myself.

I have been forced to become a new version of me. A version not all people are ready and willing to accept and not all people in my life necessarily like. I say less, I do less, I want less. I was always a homebody, but this turned it into an extreme because I do not want to spend any time away from my family. Any of us can be gone at any moment, and this loss forced me to acknowledge and accept that as a truth.

I am still figuring out who I am if I am not her mom. Still trying to justify leaving my home outside of necessities. Still trying to get through the fear and the anxiety that one of us could just be gone in a flash. I will never be who I was before, I can never be, but I am always going to work to bring the sparkle back to my eyes.

Anniversary Part Four

On the one year anniversary of Pueo's passing, I wrote out four Instagram posts. One to Kekoa, one to Lucy and two reflection pieces.

Part one:

This year we experienced our first snow, my first birthday in eight years, and our first family photo without her. We did hard things, including opening our home to love again. We hiked, and walked, and hiked some more. We renewed my parents' vows, and took our first family photo with Lucy. We watched my baby brother graduate and move into college. I grew my Bayside crew by a lot. I flew across the country to kiss the mayor and see Bayside in the desert. And I cried... a lot.

I saw a medium who connected me with her and she told me how and why she hid her illness from me. She told me where she would wait for me. She spoke to me without the medium, in dreams, in conversation. She never made me doubt that we are forever connected.

The most important thing we did? Survived. I'll never know how. I'll never understand how I didn't die right there along with her. I'll never understand the why, the how, any of it. But we survived. We survived with holes in our hearts. Everything we do, we do with her within us, around us.

Part two:

When she died, I immediately needed to learn everything I could about grief. On Monday, December 11th, my mom and I went to the mall so I could be sized for my cremation ring. During our trip, we stopped into Barnes and Noble and I went to the self help section, thinking I'd find a step by step guide on how to survive losing the love of your life. How to survive sudden loss. No surprise, there is no guidebook. You learn how to navigate it by living through it, fighting through it, living in the grief.

The phrase 'stages of grief,' to me, implies a linear process. First you're in denial, then anger, followed by bargaining and depression, then finally acceptance.

Not true.

Each stage occurs through day to day life. Sometimes all at once, sometimes you're in acceptance, then a trigger sends you straight into anger.

I spent many days in anger, more days than not. Every time I went to Target and saw a new display, a new season, a new holiday, I imagined swiping my arm across the shelves to destroy everything in my sight. I've been angry at others, even others who have lost their babies. If they had more time than me, more warning than me, it all felt like I was slighted.

My bargaining was days I spent begging the universe to take me too. Begging to be with her again.

Denial happened in the way of convincing myself I could never love again, I'll never survive this, there's no way this is real, she has to be at home, she can't be gone forever.

Depression and I became friends again. I shamelessly depend on medication to keep me level headed day to day and had to triple my dose to keep myself afloat. It's what medication is there for. Depression has kept me from all the things that help me cope. It has controlled me on many occasions.

As for acceptance, if that's the final stage I hope I never reach it. I plan to grieve her forever because I plan to love her forever.

I spent the year in grief and here are my top three lessons:

Surround yourself with safe spaces, and never lessen yourself, your grief, your emotions for anyone. People who love and support you no matter what, will. People who don't, won't.

Never say "I loved them." You love them. Present tense. If you didn't, you wouldn't be grieving.

In many cases, losing your animal companion is more difficult than losing a human in your life. Our pets are there for us day in, day out, with absolute unwavering love and support. They see our best days and our worst days and it's all the same to them.

P.S. there is no timeline, don't let anyone make you feel otherwise.

Pueo will live on in me forever. The lessons she taught me in her life and her death will be part of me until the day we are reunited. I will always grieve her and honor her. Years from now, when the first snow falls, I'll think of the days we spent frolicking around together. I'll catch a whiff of her scent, I'll pet a dog who feels just like her and it'll transport me back to feeling her. I'll pass by the emergency vet and I'll think of that fateful night, the night my life changed. The night I felt my first true heartbreak. The night my world shattered. And on these days I'll cry. On many other days I'll smile. Grief is forever. Love is forever.

Epilogue

As this journey of losing my soul dog has unfolded, I have had to face the reality of losing my family dog, Snoopy. In September 2025, just a few months before publishing, she was diagnosed with melanoma and was given a poor prognosis. Snoopy is nearly 13 years old and although we knew we would not have her forever, by all other accounts she is perfectly healthy.

So here I sit in something I have never truly experienced before — anticipatory grief. I always thought about the losses of my companion animals, but have never been face to face with the knowledge that the end is near. Being loved by an animal companion is one of the greatest gifts we could receive, but it is also the greatest heartache. Each companion teaches us something different. They are there for different phases of our lives and represent something different in our souls.

Snoopy is the one who put me back together again. In between rehoming my childhood dog and adopting Snoopy, my life felt empty, my heart broken. She healed me. She set me up for a lifetime of loving Pueo and Kekoa and Lucy.

Moving through this anticipated loss, I will learn many more lessons. Lessons on taking a back seat, supporting others while supporting myself, and many more that I am not even aware of. The loss of Pueo was MY loss. My journey, my rules. Now it is time for me to help my mom through the loss of Snoopy. The journey will not be easy, but we will make it through the loss with strength and resiliency.

I've learned a lot about grief through this process and in some ways I learned more about myself and the world around me from her death than I did in her life. My world revolved around her and I thought when she died, I would too. I could never live on without her. Little did I know, I would not only survive, but I would completely change my view on life, death and everything in between.

Throughout the writing of the blog and the book, a lot changed. Grief is always changing and evolving, and we are constantly learning new lessons. In certain chapters there were themes I wrote about that had updates and changes, and over time, they will continue to change. Not every grief journey is the same, which is why it is not linear. When I lose Kekoa and Lucy, I will grieve differently, and may possibly write another book about it. A few things will always remain the same:

1. Grief is not linear

2. We are not alone

3. We did the best we could

4. Love is eternal

Moving into a world where I know I will soon be losing Snoopy, these will be my mantras. I will write the words on sticky notes and put them on the mirror, or repeat to myself when the guilt or the anger is too much to handle. I hope something in this book spoke to you, helped you and will lead you through this everlasting journey.

Until next time. Love, Pueo.

Afterword: Lake Placid

I am sitting at Capisce Coffee in Lake Placid, NY. We are on our first family trip with Lucy, which feels fitting because we came here on our first trip with Pueo as well.

We are staying at Van Hoevenburg Cabins, the same cabins where we spent that first family trip. We arrived late at night and as I walked Kekoa and Lucy around the property, the night was still. Everyone was tucked away for the night and all I could hear was the wind blowing...and geese. The first morning, I had a hard time sleeping so I leashed up the dogs, set up the GoPro and watched the sun rise over the Adirondack mountains.

I keep walking by the Cascade cabin where we stayed with her and I can feel her spirit with us. I can see her laying in the grass, I can vividly recall the look on the delivery man's face when we had takeout delivered. She nearly scared the life out of him with her bark.

As I sit in this coffee shop and take a break from the cabin and my family, I can feel that she is always with us. When we travel, it will always be the five of us and she will keep us safe.

Last night as a storm was coming in and the wind was whipping at 50 mph, the lights started flickering. I said to myself "please Pueo don't let the lights go out." After that the winds persisted, but the lights stayed on.

This week is also a bit of a celebration. The last day of our trip will also be the day Kekoa will have officially outlived Pueo. She lived 3,040 days and Wednesday, October 21, 2025 he will be alive 3,041 days. I hope this occasion can help me relax, be less stressed about him and his health. I hope this trip to the forest with my family can heal me in similar ways that my solo trip to the desert did.

We are planning to make this our annual family trip and we will always take her with us.

***

Twenty four hours later, I am laying in bed, resting from our 3 mile walk and watching the Price is Right when the feeling creeps into my chest. It's not the feeling of pain, sorrow, and grief, but the feeling I would get when I would look into Pueo's eyes. It's the same place that hurt every day after she died. It's the place where our soul connection existed and suddenly I realized...she's here. Suddenly I could feel her everywhere like she was walking around the cabin.

I decide to take Kekoa and Lucy for a walk around the property where we are staying, bringing the GoPro we bought for this trip so I can capture some video. As I step outside, the sun is peeking through the trees, starting to set. She's there. I snap a photo and send it to my friend who responds "she's in that photo." I send it to my medium who says "she's in that photo." They both send me the photo back, circling where they see her and it is the exact same spot where I saw her when I took the photo. That photo is on the cover of this book. I look down at my watch and it's 5:00 p.m., the time she collapsed. It is also the day that Kekoa has lived as many days as she did.

We go back to the cabin, sit on the porch and Kekoa stares off into the distance toward the area I felt her, as if he feels her but cannot figure out why he can't see her. His ears are up, on alert, waiting for her return. I recognize the look on his face, I've seen it a million times. It's the same look he gives when he is waiting for my return. She's here. This is where she's been waiting for us.

I feel her around me often and I know she is always with me, but today, the feeling in my chest and the seemingly shared experience with Kekoa made it clear: this is where she will be waiting for me.

Acknowledgments

I've hated writing this book and I've loved writing it at the same time. It brings me immense sadness that I will never see her here on this earth ever again, but it brings me solace to know that this is out in the world and may reach even one person who needs it the most.

I couldn't have done this without an entire village.

To all the dogs I've ever loved and all the dogs I ever will love. Especially Kekoa, who gave me strength on my darkest days. For Petey, Posh, Neko, Quervo, Dowd, Snoopy, DOG, Kekoa and Lucy. And for one special cat, Hendrix.

To my husband, Andrew, for inspiring me every day and pushing me to become a greater version of myself. You have pushed me to write ever since we met nearly 10 years ago and I finally listened. Thank you for allowing me to grieve fully and without pause. For going along with what

I needed in these last two years, even though sometimes it meant sacrificing your own needs. For holding me together while I was completely falling apart.

To Bayside, the band that saved my life more times than I can count. I would never be here without your music.

To Shea, I could never write enough words to properly express my gratitude.

To Stefanie, thank you for always making sure I do hard things, even when I reeeeeeally did not want to.

To Mark, on all the days I cried, I could always count on you to make me laugh.

To Julianne, we are living this grief journey together, navigating day by day. I am thankful life brought me back to you.

To Carly, you literally took my dream and made it into art. I am so thankful for you.

The cover art was created in collaboration with Carly. The front and back covers feature the full image taken during our stay in Lake Placid in October 2024. A painting, hand-painted by Carly, is laid over the left half of the image, where Pueo was seen by my medium and friends. The cabin depicted is based on the Cascade Cabin where we stayed with Pueo.

To those who taught me to love the art of reading and writing. Mary Dovey, Scott Alten, and Keith Forrest. Your mentorship throughout my life and the constant confidence in my writing made me brave enough to write this, put this into the world and hopefully impact others. You all said if I applied myself, I would have straight A's. I hope this earns me that A.

To Grandmom, thank you for giving me the most perfect girl. I would never be where I am today without her... or without you.

To Matthew Flannelly, thank you for my first lesson on grief and the importance of keeping someone alive through stories and memories.

To anyone who I've impacted on Instagram or on the blog, everyone in the Anti-Cruelty Society Pet Loss Support Group, all my Bayside besties, my Discord friends and anyone else who has supported me near or far. You are all woven into these words.

And most importantly, mom. From as far back as I can remember, you have been my number one inspiration and role model. Now it's time for me to be yours. It's your turn to be published.

Resources

These are my tried and true resources, shops I trust and love, and books I've read.

Hotlines:

- 988 – National Suicide Hotline

- 607-218-7457 – Cornell School of Veterinary Medicine Hotline – student volunteer run and not always accessible. Leave a message and they call back within a few days.

Books:

- *When Things Fall Apart* by Pema Chödrön

- *Heart Dog: Surviving the Loss of Your Canine Soulmate* by Roxanne Hawn

- *The Guilt of Grief* by Alan Wolfelt – part of a series

for different experiences

- *Grief One Day at a Time* by Alan Wolfelt

- *Saying Goodbye to the Pet You Love* by Lorri Greene

Other:

- *A Tribute to My Beloved Animal* by Dr. Katie Lawlor

- *Coloring Through Grief and Loss*

- **Support groups and websites:**

- aplb.org – offers other resources and daily chat room

- https://www.amcny.org/pet-loss-support-program/ – Bi-Weekly until 3 months, monthly 3 months to one year

- Lap of Love– Offers different types of support groups and resources

- Anti-Cruelty Society support group — https://anticruelty.org/pet-loss-support — meets via Zoom on the first Tuesday and second Wednesday of each month

Etsy shops for memorial pieces:

- JinsBears

- CaitlynMinimalist

- GeoPersonalized

Other memorial:
- Kens cremation creations

Other support:
- lasagnalove.org – organization where a community member will make a lasagna and drop off to your home

- I know a psychic medium and I had a great experience with her. Here is her Etsy shop, use code PUEOSPALS15 for 15% off. https://www.etsy.com/shop/OutofAllTheStars

About the author

Briar Rose Simon is a devoted dog mom, sharing her life with her husband, Andrew, and their pups, Kekoa and Lucy. A passionate writer, she began writing to process the loss of her soul dog, translating her emotions and memories onto the page to offer comfort to others navigating grief. Becoming a published author has been a lifelong dream, and she is grateful to turn the pain of loss into a source of hope and healing. When she's not writing, Briar enjoys reality TV, seeing Bayside with her best friends, and savoring a good cup of coffee.

www.ingramcontent.com/pod-product-compliance
Lightning Source LLC
Chambersburg PA
CBHW021153130626
46554CB00005B/1802